I Am Okay to FEEL

zando young readers

A Zando Imprint

Zando
zandoprojects.com

First Edition: November 2022

Design by Carol Ly
Resources and activities by Drs. Farzana Saleem and Aubrey Harrison

The publisher does not have control over and is not responsible for author
or other third-party websites (or their content).

Library of Congress Control Number: 2022939783

978-1-63893-010-5 (Hardcover)
978-1-63893-077-8 (B&N)
978-1-63893-011-2 (ebook)

10 9 8 7 6 5 4 3 2 1
Manufactured in the United States of America

I Am Okay to FEEL

KARAMO BROWN

WITH JASON "RACHEL" BROWN

Illustrated by Diobelle Cerna

zando
young
readers
NEW YORK

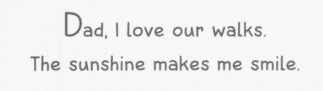

Dad, I love our walks.
The sunshine makes me smile.

It makes me smile, too.
And I love when you share your feelings.

I feel happy.

And when I'm happy,
I feel like spinning and jumping,
jumping and spinning . . .

I feel like jumping and spinning, too. When I'm really happy, like right now, I might even do a little dance.

Dance with me!

What else?

Rhinos.

Stars.

Mud puddles!

And . . . your shoes!

They make me feel happy, too.

I like the color.

But I can't see them anymore . . .

I can't see the blue sky anymore either.

It's getting dark.

And now the soft wind
is a loud wind.

When I look up at the stormy sky,
my head is filled with a million different thoughts.

**Well, did you know our thoughts
become feelings? What's in your head?**

I'm thinking, what if
I get wet and my
socks get soggy?

I'm thinking, what if it rains so hard,
we get lost in the storm?

You are okay to feel scared.
Why does the storm scare you?
I think of buildings shaking, trees touching
the ground. We might not be able to
get home—where it's safe.

What would make you feel
safe right now?

I don't know.
It's hard to think
and feel at the
same time.

Sometimes, it helps to take a deep breath first.
Will you do it with me? Breathe in and out.

Let's do it again. This time, when you breathe out,
can you make a sound as loud as the wind outside?

Whoosh!

Can you make a sound *louder* than the wind outside?

whoosh!

That's it!

It's still so loud, Dad. What if the wind blows us away?
Can you feel your feet in your shoes? Wiggle your toes.
Feel how solid the ground is beneath your feet.

I think I know what will make me feel better.
I'm listening.

I'll feel better when I can't hear or feel the wind,
when I can't see the lightning or hear the thunder.

We can't stop the wind, or the lightning,
or the thunder. But I promise it won't be forever.

No storm lasts forever.

I just want to be in a quiet place.
Someplace warm and safe.
I want to go home.

We're not home yet, but look . . .
it's quiet and warm and safe here.

I'm with you.

Whenever I start to feel a little better,
I stand up and stretch my arms high into the sky,

like I am a tree that
can't be moved . . .

Then I stretch my arms out
beside me like I'm a star!

I push my chest out like I am the sun
and I am putting out sunshine rays.
This is fun, Dad! I feel so much better.
Movement can help us feel better.

Dad, we made it
through the storm. You were right.
Storms don't last forever.

But look . . .

But see . . . the sky is still the sky, the trees are still the trees,
the ground is still the ground, firm beneath your feet.
Our home is safe because we make it safe, for each other.

Dad, I feel silly about being
scared earlier . . .

. . . which then makes me
feel mad that I didn't
act like a big kid.

Your feelings are never silly. We feel what we feel.

You should never feel embarrassed
or mad about having feelings.

Really, Dad?

Yep! Even if others try to make you feel like
your feelings are silly, which might hurt . . .

Remember what
we did earlier.

Take a deep breath in and out.

**Remind yourself, I am okay to feel
scared, happy, angry, or sad.**

Yes, you are!

RESOURCES & ACTIVITIES

developed by Dr. Farzana Saleem and Dr. Aubrey Harrison

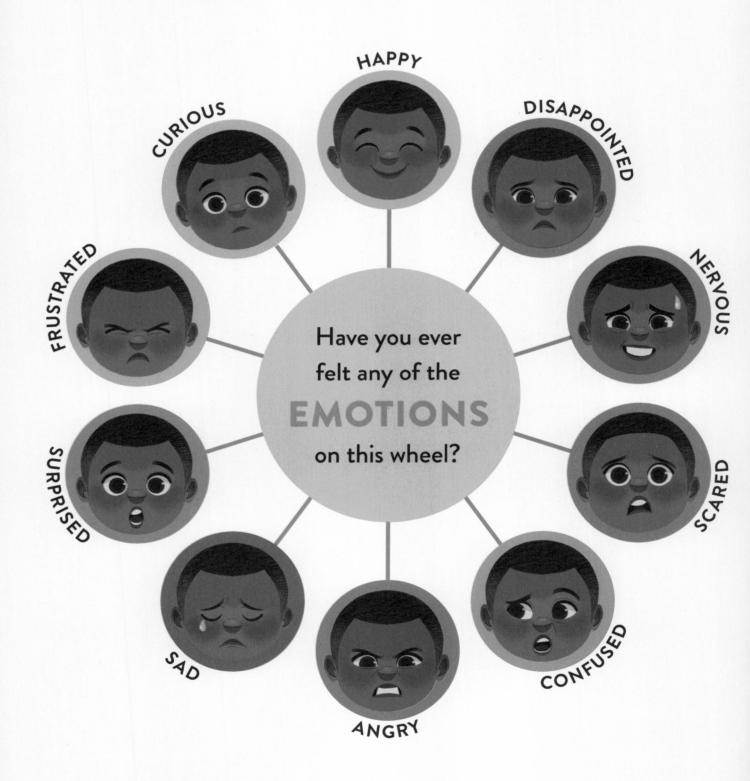

Have you ever felt any of the **EMOTIONS** on this wheel?

HAPPY
CURIOUS
DISAPPOINTED
FRUSTRATED
NERVOUS
SURPRISED
SCARED
SAD
ANGRY
CONFUSED

Let's try an activity that helps us become more aware of how our feelings change our faces. The way we communicate our emotions is often through our facial expressions.

1   Point to a face on the wheel that you want
    your parent or caregiver to make.
    When your parent makes that face, what do you see?
    Are they smiling or frowning?
    How did it make you feel when they made that face?

2   Now it's your turn!
    Pick a face on the wheel and make that face.
    Ask your parent or caregiver to describe what they see.
    How did that make you feel when you made that face?

3   Pick a face on the wheel and describe a time
    when you've made that face.
    How did you feel? What made you feel that way?
    Now pick two more faces and repeat the activity.

The next time you are feeling an emotion, you can show your parent or caregiver the Emotions Wheel and tell them why you feel that way.

Thoughts, Feelings & Behavior Cycle

Our thoughts are connected to our emotions, which are then connected to our behavior. Jason shared a lot of his thoughts and feelings with his father in the story, and we saw how those thoughts and feelings changed his behaviors.

Thought: "I love our walks." ⟶ **Feeling: Happy** ⟶ **Behavior:**

Thought: "What if it rained so hard that we got lost in the storm?" ⟶ **Feeling: Worried** ⟶ **Behavior:**

Let's Talk!

- How did feeling happy change Jason's actions? How did feeling worried change Jason's feelings and actions?
- Can you point to Jason's feelings on the Emotions Wheel?
- Can you show Jason's feelings on your own face?
- Has there ever been a time when you felt happy or worried?
- What's a thought that makes you feel happy? How did you show how you feel?
- What's a thought that makes you feel worried? How did you show how you feel?

Let's Feel It Out!

Here are some steps that you and your parent or caregiver can use when you may not know how to express how you're feeling.

Your parent or caregiver can **F.E.E.L.**

✓ **F** ind out where the feeling is coming from,

✓ **E** mbrace the emotions that are present,

✓ **E** ngage in 10 seconds of deep breathing, and

✓ **L** earn your child's emotional cues.

Remember, when you have big or difficult emotions, it's **O.K.A.Y.**

✓ **O** ffer your feelings to an adult by sharing how you feel.

✓ **K** eep taking deep breaths, and

✓ **A** sk an adult for help to calm you down because

✓ **Y** our feelings matter!

Dear Reader,

When I was growing up, I had so many emotions that were big and small. As a child, I didn't know how to talk through my emotions, so I would often try to hide them. But ignoring my feelings didn't make anything better, and I would sometimes express my emotions in a non-healthy manner. But with patience and love, my father taught me that it is important to feel your feelings, and how I should open up about my emotions to the people that cared about me.

My father and I wrote this book together to share the many lessons he gave me to give to you. We wanted to show you how to love yourself and your emotions, and the big and small ways you can find comfort during stressful times—whether it's jumping in mud puddles, talking to a parent, or coming up with a silly dance! We hope that this is just the beginning of many conversations you'll have about your emotions!

—JASON "RACHEL" BROWN

Remember, you are okay to feel . . . and to heal!

—KARAMO BROWN